BREAK DANCES

Michael Baroff

With Love

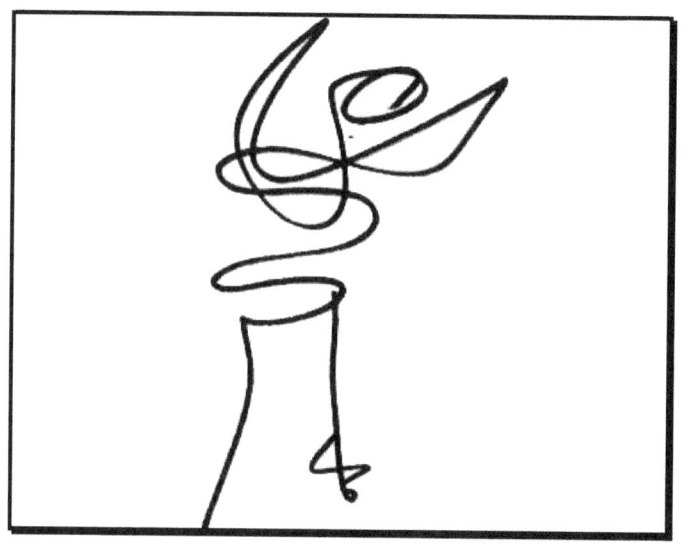

Break Fast

After a hiatus
Back into the scene
Ready to meet you

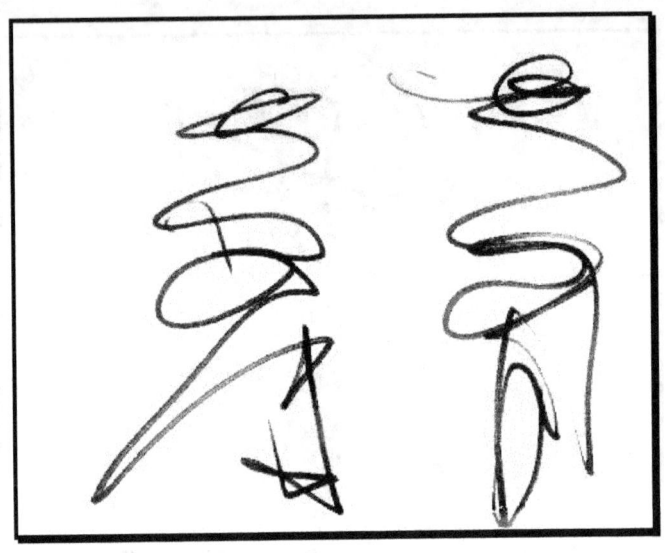

Break Ice

First time meeting
Relaxed and present
Say all the right words

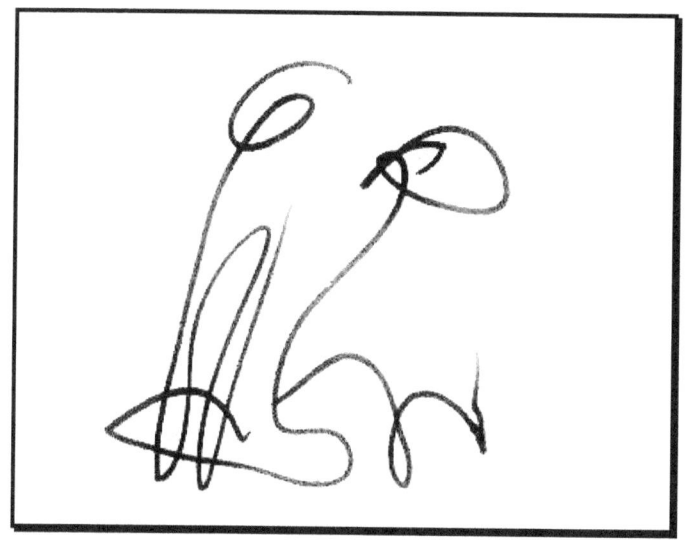

Break Bread

Sit down to a meal
Look into your eyes
Get to know each other

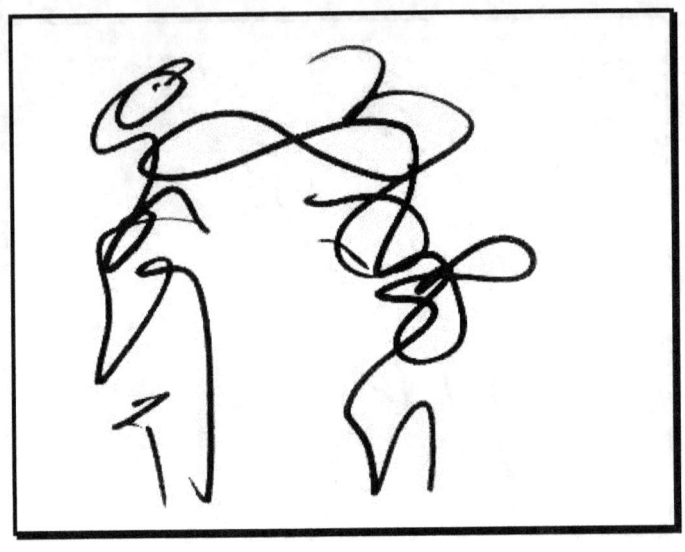

Break In

Defenses down
Open to possibilities
Test our boundaries

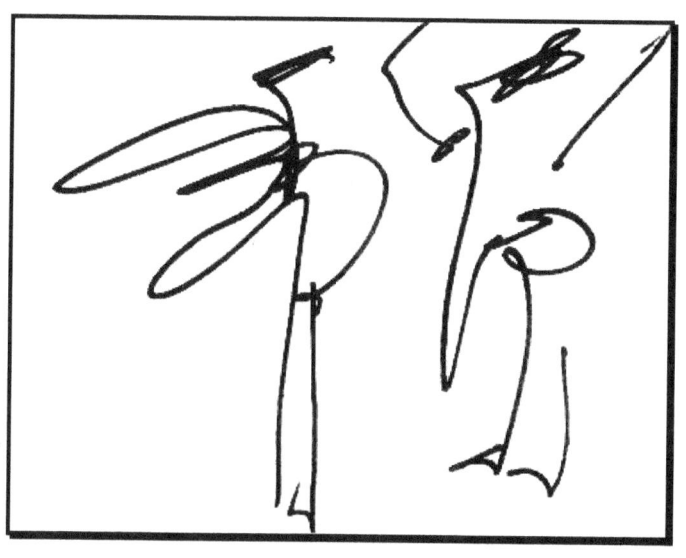

Break On

Too much
Too fast
Too soon

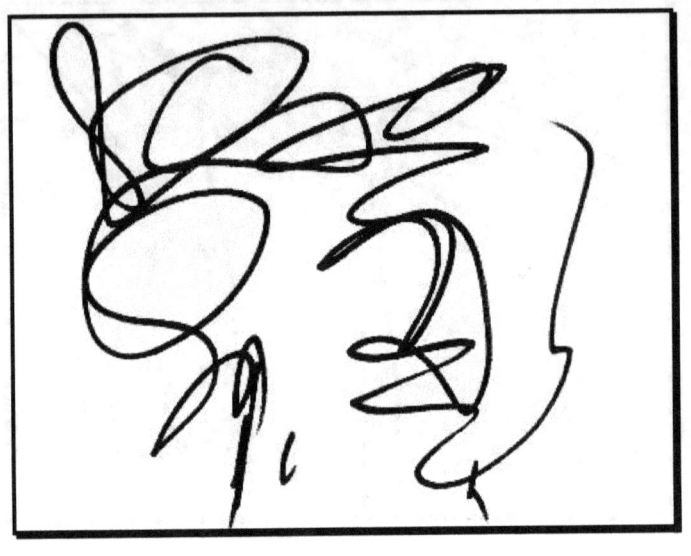

Break Stride

Obstacles appear
Choices to make
Into, through, around

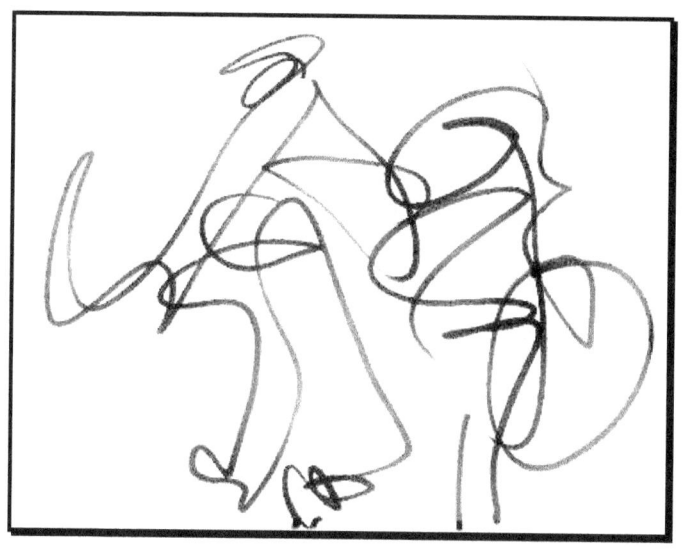

Break Down

Fears expressed
Emotions released
Ingredients for intimacy

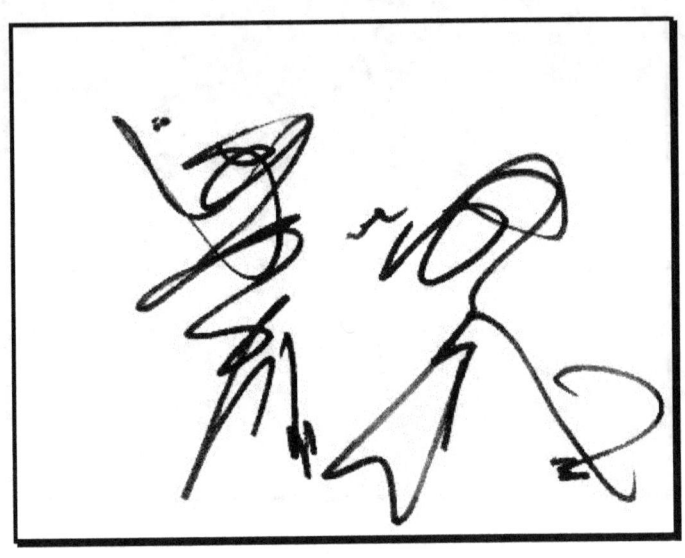

Break Up

It's not you or me
It's both of us
Not right, not now

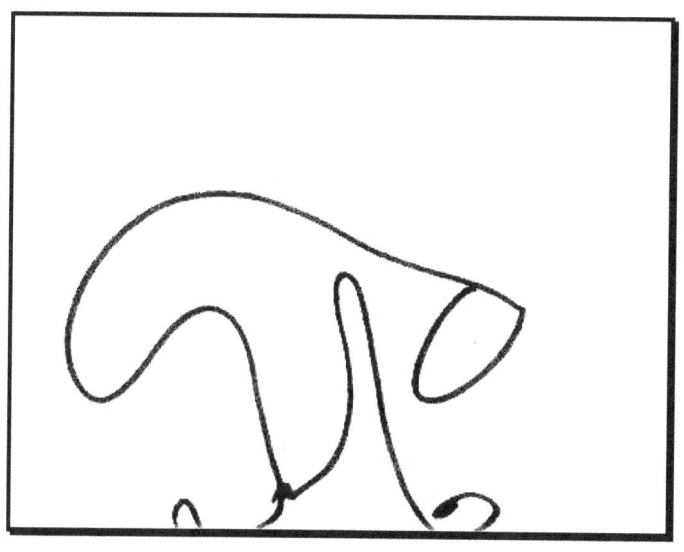

Break Heart

Disconnected
Disappointed
Dispirited

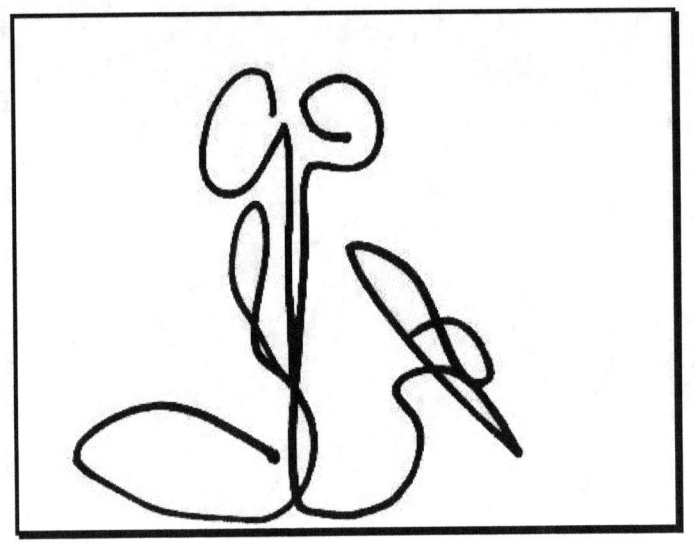

Break Off

Separate
Feel the hurt
Listen to our hearts

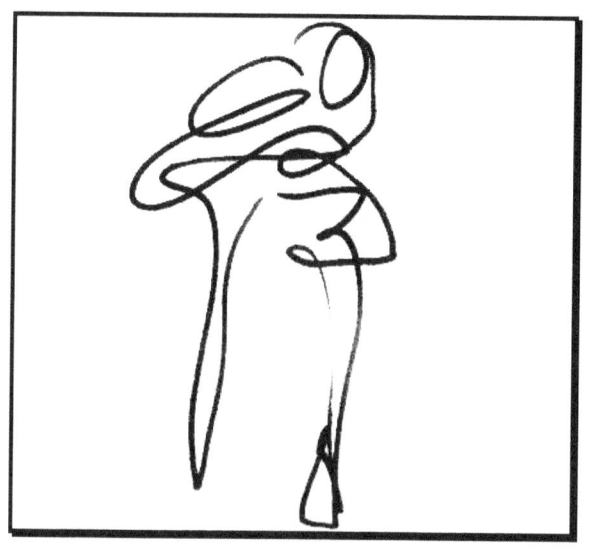

Break Ground

Insight revealed
Greater understanding
Deeper connection

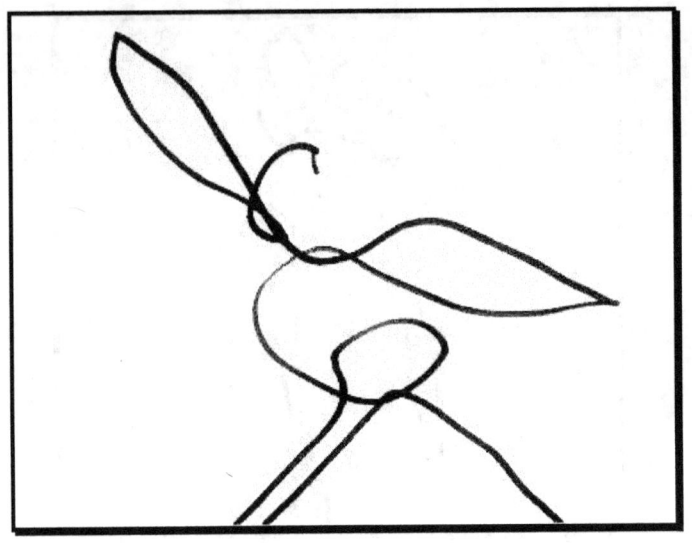

Break Out

Let go
Get down
Keep moving

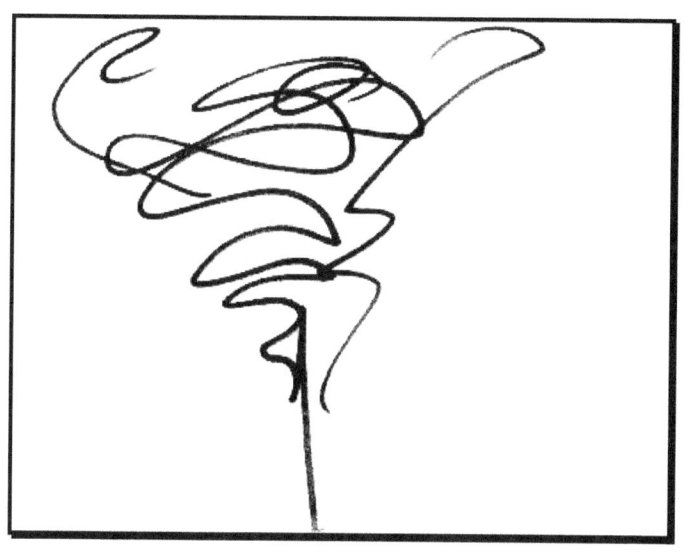

Take a Break

Reconnect to self
Nothing to possess
Get grounded

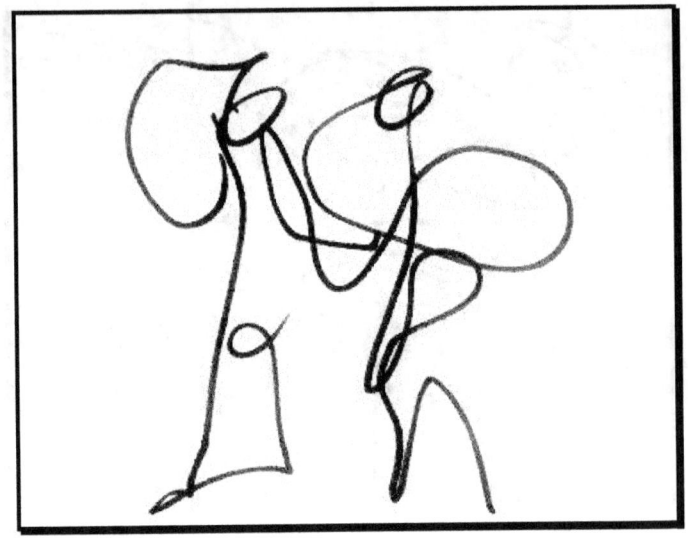

Break Cover

Emerge from hiding
Provide support
Everything to gain

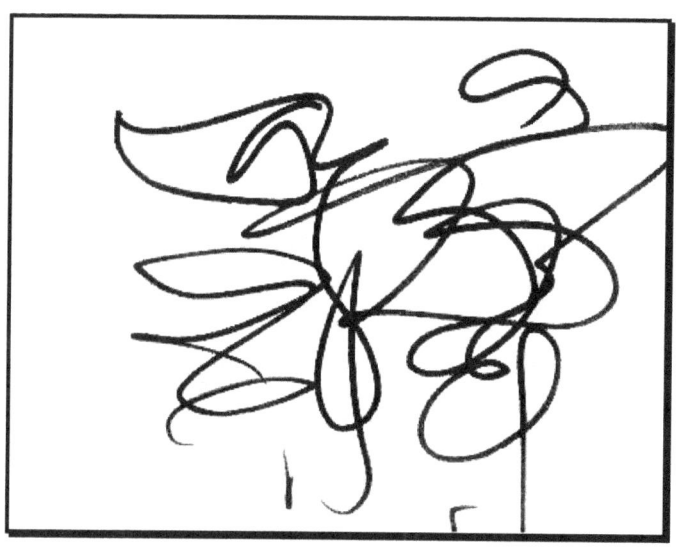

Break Through

Uncover another layer
New perspective gained
Being together again

Michael Baroff
Santa Monica, California

www.IWOW.biz

www.MetascapeArt.com